THE XXL MEDITERRANEAN DIET COOKBOOK FOR UK

Delicious and Easy-Going Recipes for Every Day incl. 14 Days MD Weight Loss Plan

FOOD CLUB UK

TABLE OF CONTENTS

Introduction

These days we're all far more concerned with health and fitness than ever before.

This isn't a bad thing by any means. Being healthy means that you're drastically reducing your risk factors for serious disease and you're giving yourself a chance to live far longer than if you insisted on living in an unhealthy way.

However, health and fitness is a loose term. Health means something to one person and another thing to another. That's why it's important to have a clear vision of what will take you towards a healthier lifestyle in general.

Your diet is without a doubt one of the most important aspects of your health and fitness plan. You can exercise all you like but if you're eating unhealthy foods far too often, you're not going to lose weight, keep it off, or reduce your risk factors for serious health concerns, such as diabetes, heart disease, obesity, etc.

There are countless diets out there, but we all know that the fad diet route simply doesn't work.

A fad diet is a diet which is extremely restrictive and leaves you having to count calories to the extreme, weigh out ingredient strictly, or have days which are dedicated to colours and food types. All of this becomes a difficult situation to follow and it ties you up in knots. It's also extremely restrictive and that leaves you craving all the foods that you wish you could eat. Soon, something has to give, and that's normally your resolve. You end up bingeing simply because you can, meaning that the diet is over and you feel terrible as a result.

Surely it's a far better option to find a healthy, sustainable lifestyle, rather than a diet?

In this book we're going to talk about something called the Mediterranean Diet. Now, the word 'diet' is in the title, but this isn't really a diet and it's far more towards the healthy lifestyle side of the scale. When you opt to live the Mediterranean way, you're limiting your intake of unhealthy foods and you're maximising your intake of the healthy stuff. You're also focusing on clean and whole foods and banishing processed rubbish from your life.

Of course, exercise is also important alongside your diet, but when you're giving your body what it needs to function correctly and effectively, everything else becomes easier.

So, what exactly is the Mediterranean Diet?

What Is The Mediterranean Diet?

The Mediterranean Diet, as the name suggests, links back to the Mediterranean region, especially Italy, Spain, and France, and Greece. In these countries, there is an abundance of fresh produce and as such, daily diets are based around that produce. The diet was first introduced in the 1960s and since then it has been adapted many different times.

However, the basic Mediterranean Diet is very similar to a regular healthy eating lifestyle in general, which makes it one of the easiest to follow and one of the most effective, and healthiest all around.

The diet is full of fresh vegetables, fresh fruit, nuts, beans, legumes, grains, fresh fish, cereals and fats which are unsaturated, especially olive oil. In these regions, olive oil is used in abundance and this has many health benefits including boosting heart health and, of course, adding flavour to dishes.

With this diet, there is no weighing of ingredients, no counting calories or carbs, and nothing particularly difficult at all. That means that it is easy to follow over the long term and gives you a far healthier outlook, and a more sustainable choice as a result.

The good news is that foods such as bread, pasta, and rice, which are often ruled out in some diets, are completely fine to eat on the Mediterranean Diet, as long as you opt for the wholegrain versions. These foods are staples in Mediterranean countries and they're used to fill up on, therefore meaning that you eat far less than you otherwise would, and you don't feel hungry a couple of hours later.

The Do's And Don'ts of The Mediterranean Diet

The Mediterranean Diet varies depending upon the source you take it from however, it has some basic principles. Let's look at the do eats and don't eats when following this healthy lifestyle.

Do eat:

- ✓ Fresh vegetables
- ✓ Olives
- ✓ Fresh fruits
- ✓ Nuts, such as almonds, walnuts, macadamia nuts and hazelnuts in particular
- ✓ Seeds, such as sunflower and pumpkin seeds
- ✓ Potatoes, including sweet potatoes
- ✓ Legumes, e.g. peas, beans, lentils, pulses, chickpeas peanuts
- ✓ Wholegrains, such as whole oats, barley, brown rice, wholegrain pasta
- ✓ Bread, as long as it is wholegrain/brown bread
- ✓ Herbs
- ✓ Fresh fish, such as sardines, salmon, tuna, mackerel, trout, mussels, crab and shrimp in particular
- ✓ Seafood
- ✓ Spices
- ✓ Olive oil, particularly the extra virgin variety
- ✓ Avocados and avocado oil
- ✓ Plenty of water
- ✓ 1 glass of red wine per day
- ✓ Coffee and tea, as long as you don't sweeten them

You can also eat the following with a few restrictions:

- ✓ Eggs – in moderation
- ✓ Cheese – in moderation
- ✓ Yogurt (including Greek yogurt) – in moderation

- ✓ Chicken and other poultry products – in moderation
- ✓ Red meat – occasionally

You should avoid eating:

- ✓ Processed meat products, such as hot dogs or packaged burgers, etc
- ✓ Other foods which are processed, such as 'low fat' foods or anything which is labelled as 'diet'
- ✓ Refined oils, such as canola oil, soybean oil, etc
- ✓ Refined grains, such as white bread
- ✓ Trans fats, including margarine
- ✓ Anything which contains added sugars, such as ice cream, candies, etc
- ✓ Beverages which are sweetened with sugar, such as cola

As you can see, the Mediterranean Diet is basically a healthy lifestyle which makes use of fresh produce that is readily available in Mediterranean countries. The good news is that these products are readily available worldwide, including in the UK. Make sure that the bulk of your diet is made up of fresh fruits and vegetables, aiming to get a good amount every single day.

You are able to snack, but again, make sure these are healthy snacks which are within the 'do' list of foods above. Fresh fruits or nuts/seeds are a great and healthy go-to which will give you plenty of vitamins and minerals, as well as healthy fats.

How to Prepare Your Kitchen For The Mediterranean Diet

One of the best things about following the Mediterranean Diet is that you don't need any specific equipment. You simply need to get rid of anything deemed unhealthy and make sure you stock up your fridge and cupboards with the healthy stuff. You also don't need to do any weighing of ingredients or counting. This is partly why this diet is a particularly good option for busy people or those who have found other diets hard to stick to in the past.

Preparing your kitchen before you begin the diet means that you're far more likely to stick to it. Go through your cupboards, fridge, and freezer and get rid of anything sugary or processed. Basically, anything which is on the 'do not eat' list outlined above needs to go. You can gift this to a friend or neighbour, or you can donate it to a food bank – don't throw it away!

Don't be tempted to keep sugary snacks in the kitchen for special occasions or for the kids. This will simply mean that you're more likely to fall foul of them when you're having a sugar craving. These will come, no matter what type of diet you're on!

Instead, make plenty of space for healthy options and look for healthy snacks whenever you feel the need to indulge a little.

Here are a few other tips to get your Mediterranean Diet journey off to a good start:

- ✓ **Plan your first week's meals a day or two before you're going to start** – This will give you more time to focus on other things and means you're not going to have to sit down and wonder what to make for dinner. When you have less time, you're more likely to fall into old patterns. Planning is key, especially at first. Handily, at the end of the book you'll find a meal plan you might like to follow at the start.

- ✓ **Buy all of your week's ingredients** – Once you've planned out your week's worth of meals, write a shopping list and purchase all the ingredients you need. Some of these you might already have, such as olive oil, garlic, spices, etc, but if not, stock up at the start and these will last you a good amount of time.

- ✓ **Buy organic produce if possible** – Organic produce is healthier, packed with vitamins and minerals and fits into the Mediterranean Diet perfectly. It's possible to purchase organic produce cheaper than you think; many supermarkets have an organic section nowadays and if you shop for deals or discounts, you'll find some bargains. You can freeze many vegetables for use later on, so that is something to consider if you're worried about them spoiling towards the end of the week.

- ✓ **Don't shop when you're hungry** – Whether you're shopping in person at the supermarket or you're doing your online shop from your living room, do not do this whilst you're hungry! All you'll end up doing is buying too much or buying things that you shouldn't be eating. Make sure that you're comfortably full and simply buy what you need. That way, you'll save money too.

- ✓ **Remember to read food labels** – There are many hidden ingredients in foods that you may not be aware of. You need to learn to read food labels to avoid falling foul of unhealthy ingredients without even realising it. Also, remember that anything labelled as 'low fat' or 'diet' needs to be avoided. These items have been processed to make them low in fat or fit for a particular diet and that's not what the Mediterranean Diet is about. These foods also often contain artificial sugars for sweetening purposes.

- ✓ **Mix up your meals** – Finally, remember to mix up your meals from day to day and don't fall into patterns of eating the same thing all the time. Throughout this book you'll find many delicious recipes you can try that fit in perfectly with the Mediterranean Diet. That means you can create different dishes on a daily basis and not become bored with your diet. Of course, this also means you're more likely to stick to it.

- ✓ **Make sure you drink enough water** – Water is a big must do on the Mediterranean Diet so make sure that you keep a refillable bottle with you at all times and try and finish it. There is no right or wrong amount of water you should be drinking per day, but the goal is to drink whenever you're thirsty, or to avoid becoming thirsty in the first place! Around 8 glasses per day is the recommended amount, but again, this varies.

- ✓ **Stop eating when you're full** – Another key thing to remember when following this diet is that when you're full, you need to stop eating. Put down that knife, fork, or spoon, and stop. Learn to recognise the signs that you're hungry by eating slowly, chewing your food carefully, and tuning in to how you feel. It's never a bad thing to learn how to eat more mindfully!

As you can see, the Mediterranean Diet isn't a difficult one. You'll also find as you move through the recipes in this book that you'll never be bored or at a loss as to what to eat on a daily basis!

So, if you're ready to begin your journey into the Mediterranean lifestyle, let's get started!

Mediterranean Diet Recipes

From fish to chicken, soup to dessert, we've got you covered with a whole range of delicious Mediterranean Diet dishes to create, starting right now!

Breakfast Recipes

Artichoke & Spinach Breakfast Frittata

Serves 4

Calories – 263, carbs – 21.1g, protein – 10.4g, fat – 15.9g

Ingredients

- 1 tbsp Dijon mustard
- 10 large eggs
- 2 tbsp olive oil
- 125g sour cream
- 1 tsp salt
- 0.25 tsp black pepper
- 2 minced garlic cloves
- 250g grated cheese
- 500g baby spinach
- 5 artichoke hearts, quartered and chopped

Method

1. Preheat your oven to 200 C
2. Take a large mixing bowl and add the sour cream, mustard, eggs, seasonings, and half of the cheese. Combine well and place to one side
3. Take a large skillet and add the oil, heating over a medium setting
4. Add the artichokes and cook until they're slightly brown, which should take around 8 minutes
5. Add the garlic and spinach and combine
6. Cook for around 2 minutes
7. Arrange the contents of the pan into one even layer and pour the egg mixture over the top
8. Sprinkle the rest of the cheese over the top
9. Heat the pan for a few minutes, until the edges of the eggs start to cook
10. Place the pan into the oven for around 15 minutes, until the eggs have set
11. Allow to cool for a few minutes and cut into slices

Breakfast Shakshuka

Serves 4

Calories – 454, carbs – 19g, protein – 12g, fat – 14.5g

Ingredients

- 1 can peeled tomatoes
- 1 chopped onion
- 2 tbsp olive oil
- 1 tbsp harissa paste
- 3 minced garlic cloves
- 2 tbsp tomato paste
- 1 tsp cumin
- 6 eggs
- 0.5 tsp salt
- A handful of cilantro leaves, shredded

Method

1. Take a large bowl and pour the tomatoes inside. Take a fork and crush the contents of the bowl until small. Place to one side
2. Take a large skillet and add the oil, heating over a medium temperature
3. Add the onion and cook for a few minutes, until translucent
4. Add the garlic, cumin, tomato paste, harissa paste, and the salt, combining well and cooking for around a minute
5. Add the tomatoes and allow the pan contents to simmer for around 10 minutes, until the sauce has thickened
6. Remove the pan from the heat
7. Create six holes in the mixture and crack one egg into each hole
8. Distribute a little of the sauce over the top of the eggs, but only over the whites
9. Place the pan back on the heat and cook for around 12 minutes, until the eggs are cooked to your particular liking
10. Sprinkle the cilantro over the top before serving

Sprout & Sweet Potato Hash

Serves 2

Calories – 206, carbs – 19, protein – 10g, fat – 11g

Ingredients

- 400g Brussels sprouts, cut into quarters
- 1 sweet potato, cut into cubes
- 1 tbsp avocado oil for the potatoes and another 2 tsp for the rest
- 1 small, chopped onion
- 2 minced cloves of garlic
- 400g chopped apple
- 1 tbsp dried sage
- 4 eggs
- 250g fresh spinach
- Salt and pepper for seasoning

Method

1. Preheat your oven to 200 C
2. Take a baking sheet and line with parchment paper
3. Add the Brussels sprouts and the potatoes to the baking sheet and drizzle 1 tbsp of the avocado oil over the top, distributing evenly
4. Season and give everything a good shake to coat
5. Place in the oven for 25 minutes, shaking the sheet at the halfway mark
6. Take a large skillet pan and heat over a medium temperature
7. Add the rest of the oil ad add the apple, sage, and garlic
8. Cook for 3 minutes until fragrant
9. Add the cooked sweet potato and Brussels sprouts and combine
10. Remove from the heat and set to one side
11. Take another skillet and add a small amount of oil
12. Cook the four eggs to your particular liking – you can either fry them or scramble them
13. Serve the eggs on top of the hash and serve hot

Scrambled Eggs, Med Style

Serves 1

Calories – 249, carbs – 13g, protein – 17g, fat – 14g

Ingredients

- 1 tbsp olive oil
- 2 sliced spring onions
- 1 sliced yellow pepper
- 2 tbsp black peppers, de-stoned and sliced
- 8 quartered cherry tomatoes
- 1 tbsp capers
- 0.25 tsp oregano, dried
- 4 medium eggs
- Salt and pepper to season

Method

1. Take a large frying pan and add the oil, heating over a medium temperature
2. Add the spring onions and peppers and cook until soft
3. Add the olives, capers, and tomatoes and cook for a further minute
4. Add the eggs into the pan and use a spoon to scramble them quickly
5. Add the oregano and season to your liking
6. Keep scrambling and stirring your eggs until they're as cooked as you like

Mediterranean Morning Casserole

Serves 4

Calories – 196, carbs – 5g, protein – 10g, fat – 12g

Ingredients

- 450ml fresh milk
- 12 eggs
- 2 minced garlic cloves
- 400g spinach, fresh works best but frozen would work too
- 4 artichoke hearts, chopped
- 250g crumbled feta cheese
- 1 tbsp chopped dill, fresh
- 1 tsp lemon juice
- 1 tsp dried oregano
- 4 tsp olive oil
- Salt and pepper for seasoning

Method

1. Preheat your oven to 190 C
2. Chop up the artichoke hearts
3. Take a large skillet and add 1 tbsp olive oil
4. Over a medium heat, sauté the garlic and spinach for around 3 minutes
5. Take a large baking dish and create a layer of spinach and artichoke in the bottom
6. Take a medium mixing bowl and add the eggs, herbs, lemon juice, milk and seasoning, combining well
7. Pour the mixture over the spinach and artichoke, moving the dish around to coat evenly
8. Crumble the feta cheese over the top, distributing evenly
9. Place in the oven for around 35 minutes, until cooked throughout

Breakfast Pizza

Serves 2

Calories – 873, carbs – 43g, protein – 36g, fat – 62g

Ingredients

- 2 tbsp olive oil
- Quarter of a chopped onion
- 4 slices of bacon
- 4 beaten eggs
- 2 pitta rounds
- 2 tbsp pesto
- Half a chopped tomato
- 3 chopped mushrooms
- A handful of spinach leaves
- 200g grated cheddar cheese
- 1 sliced, pitted, and peeled avocado

Method

1. Preheat your oven to 175 C
2. Take a baking sheet and line with baking parchment
3. Take a large skillet and cook the bacon over a medium heat, turning after 5 minutes and cooking for 10 minutes in total
4. Pat the bacon dry on paper towels
5. Using the same skillet, cook the onion for around 5 minutes
6. Remove the onion and place to one side
7. Add the olive oil to the skillet
8. Add the eggs and cook for around 4 minutes, stirring every so often
9. Add the pitta bread to your baking sheet
10. Spread a little pesto over each pitta
11. Add a little bacon on top of the pesto
12. Add the egg mixture and then add the tomato, spinach and the mushroom
13. Top the pitta with a little cheese and season to your liking
14. Place the baking sheet into the oven and cook for around 10 minutes
15. Serve alongside the sliced avocado

Hummus With Cauliflower Fritters

Serves 2

Calories – 333, carbs – 45g, protein – 14g, fat – 13g

Ingredients

- 2.5 tbsp olive oil (separate for frying)
- 1 can of chickpeas
- 2 tbsp minced garlic
- 1 chopped onion
- Half a cauliflower head, cut into small cubes
- 2 tbsp hummus
- Salt and pepper for seasoning

Method

1. Preheat your oven to 220 C
2. Take the chickpeas and drain and rinse, drying them on a paper towel
3. Take a large bowl and place the chickpeas inside
4. Add 1 tbsp olive oil and toss to coat
5. Take a large baking tray and line with parchment paper
6. Lay the chickpeas on the tray, making sure they don't overlap and season well
7. Place in the oven for 20 minutes, stirring occasionally
8. Remove from the oven and place the chickpeas n a food processor, creating a crumbly textured mixture, set aside
9. Take a medium frying pan and add the rest of the olive oil over a medium heat
10. Add the garlic and onion and cook for 2 minutes
11. Add the cauliflower and cook for another 2 minutes, stirring occasionally
12. Cover the pan and turn the heat down a little, cooking until the cauliflower is tender
13. Place the cauliflower mixture into the food processer and half of the chickpea crumbs you made earlier
14. Combine and pulse together lightly
15. Take a large frying pan and add just a little oil to coat, heating over a medium temperature
16. Form patties out of the cauliflower mixture and cook on each side for around 3 minutes, until golden brown
17. Serve with the hummus on top

Delicious Breakfast Quinoa

Serves 4
Calories – 327, carbs – 53g, protein – 11g, fat – 7.9g

Ingredients

- 150g chopped almonds (raw)
- 150g quinoa
- 250ml milk
- 2 tbsp honey
- 1 tsp cinnamon
- 1 tsp vanilla extract
- 5 chopped apricots (dried)
- 2 chopped dates (dried)
- Pinch of salt

Method

1. Take a large skillet pan and toast the almonds for around 5 minutes
2. Remove the almonds from the skillet and place to one side
3. Take a medium saucepan and add the quinoa and cinnamon, stirring over a medium heat for a few minutes, until just warm
4. Add the milk and salt and combine well
5. Bring the contents of the pan to the boil and then reduce down to low
6. Cover the pan and simmer for 15 minutes
7. Add the honey, apricots, dates, vanillas and the almonds into the quinoa and combine well

Caprese Breakfast Muffin

Serves 2

Calories – 186, carbs – 28.8g, protein – 16.3g, fat – 1.5g

Ingredients

- 2 wholewheat muffins, split into two
- 2 chunky slices of fresh tomato
- 2 egg whites
- A handful of spinach leaves

Method

1. Take a non-stick frying pan and cook the egg whites for around 3-4 minutes, until translucent
2. Meanwhile, toast the muffins to your liking
3. Split the egg whites between the two bottom sections of the muffins
4. Add a little spinach to each, a tomato slice to each, and season to your liking
5. Top with the muffin lid and enjoy

Easy Egg Zucchini

Serves 2

Calories – 213, carbs – 11.2g, protein – 10.2g, fat – 15.7g

Ingredients

- 1.5 tbsp olive oil
- 2 eggs
- 2 zucchinis, cut into large cubes
- A little water
- Salt and pepper for seasoning

Method

1. Take a large skillet and add the oil over a medium heat
2. Cook the zucchini until soft, for about 10 minutes
3. Season and ensure everything is well coated
4. Take a medium bowl and beat the eggs
5. Add a very small amount of water to loosen the eggs and beat again
6. Pour the egg mixture over the zucchini
7. Stir the eggs to scramble and cook to your liking
8. Season once more and enjoy

Lunch Recipes

Simple Pasta Salad

Serves 1

Calories – 567, carbs – 70g, protein – 22g, fat – 20g

Ingredients

- 🍽 0.5 tbsp olive oil
- 🍽 85g wholewheat pasta
- 🍽 Quarter of a chopped red onion
- 🍽 Zest and juice of half a lemon
- 🍽 100g quartered cherry tomatoes
- 🍽 Quarter of a chopped cucumber
- 🍽 60g crumbled feta cheese
- 🍽 15g chopped basil
- 🍽 Salt and pepper for seasoning

Method

1. Cook the pasta according to instructions
2. Take a small bowl and add the lemon juice and zest, the oil red onion and seasoning, combining well
3. Drain the pasta and cool with cold water
4. Place the pasta in a bowl and cover with the dressing, combining well
5. Add the tomatoes, basil, cucumber and feta over the top and combine again

Fully Stuffed Peppers

Serves 2

Calories – 373, carbs – 17g, protein – 14g, fat – 17g

Ingredients

- 1 tbsp olive oil
- 50g wholegrain rice
- 1 red pepper
- 1 yellow pepper
- 1 sliced onion
- 1 diced courgette
- 2 crushed garlic cloves
- 75g cherry tomatoes, cut into halves
- Zest of half an orange
- 1 tsp cumin
- 1 tsp coriander, ground
- 3 tbsp flat leave parsley, chopped
- 100g goat's cheese, cut into chunks
- Salt and pepper for seasoning

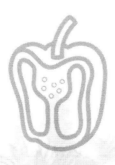

Method

1. Preheat the oven to 200 C
2. Cook the rice according to instructions and drain well
3. Take the red and yellow pepper and cut into halves, straight down the middle. Cut out the seeds
4. Cover a baking tray with parchment paper and arrange the peppers on top, with the open side upwards
5. Place into the oven for 15 minutes
6. Take a large frying pan and add the oil over a medium heat
7. Cook the courgette and onions until soft and brown, stirring every so often
8. Add the garlic, tomatoes, coriander and cumin and combine well
9. Cook for one minute
10. Pour the contents of the pan into a bowl and add the orange zest, combining once more
11. Add the parsley and the cooked rice and combine
12. Season and combine again
13. Spoon the rice mixture into the peppers
14. Add a little cheese on top of each one and place back into the oven for 10 minutes

Healthy Tuna Wraps

Serves 2
Calories – 461, carbs – 45g, protein – 39g, fat – 14g

Ingredients

- 2 egg
- 2 tbsp mayonnaise
- 50g green beans, prepared
- 4 small, sliced gherkins
- 1 tbsp drained capers
- 1 can of tuna (spring water)
- 0.25 tsp mixed herbs (dried)
- 1 sliced tomato
- 200g black olives
- 2 wholewheat tortillas
- Salt and pepper for seasoning

Method

1. Cook the beans in a pan of boiling water for around 4 minutes
2. Remove the beans from the water and place them in a bowl of cold water
3. Drain the beans and place to one side
4. Boil the egg in boiling water for 8 minutes
5. Once cooked, place the egg in cold water to cool
6. Take a medium bowl and combine the mayonnaise with the herbs, capers and the gherkin, seasoning well
7. Add the tuna and combine once more
8. Remove the egg from the cold water and remove the sheet, cutting into quarters
9. Take the tortillas and add the spinach layers on each one
10. Add the green beans on top
11. Add the mixture on top of the tortillas
12. Add the egg and then the pieces of tomato
13. Flatten the olives a little and place those on top of the tortillas
14. Fold the bottom of the wrap inwards and roll up

Vegetable Couscous With Halloumi Cheese

Serves 4

Calories – 433, carbs – 16g, protein – 14g, fat – 15.6g

Ingredients

- Olive oil cooking spray
- 150g couscous
- 1 red pepper, seeded and cut into slices
- 1 yellow pepper, seeded and cut into slices
- 1 green pepper, seeded and cut into slices
- 1 sliced red onion
- 1 sliced courgette
- 250g halloumi cheese
- 2 tbsp red wine vinegar
- 1 tbsp cornflour, mixed together with 1 tbsp water
- 1 tsp garlic powder
- 0.5 tsp dried herbs
- 2 tbsp chopped parsley leaves
- Salt and pepper for seasoning

Method

1. Take a large mixing bowl and add the couscous
2. Add a little seasoning and add the vegetable stock, combining well
3. Cover the bowl with cling film and place to one side
4. Take a large mixing bowl, add the red wine vinegar, garlic powder, herbs and salt, along with 200ml water
5. Heat the pan to a simmer
6. Remove the pan from the heat and add the cornflour paste
7. Combine and add back onto the heat, cooking for 2 minutes
8. Allow to cool before adding the parsley and combining
9. Take another large bowl and add the vegetables, seasoning with salt and pepper and ensuring everything is combined
10. Take a large griddle pan and spray with cooking spray over a high heat
11. Place half of the vegetables onto the pan and spray them with the cooking oil
12. Cook for around 5 minutes and then turn over and cook for another 5 minutes
13. Remove and repeat the process with the rest of the vegetables
14. Take the halloumi and cut into halves, adding up to six slices
15. Cook the halloumi on the griddle pan, creating char lines and cooking for 6minutes on each side
16. Take the cooled couscous and mix through with a fork
17. Add the vegetables and the halloumi and combine
18. Add the dressing over the top and combine once more

Fresh Panzanella

Serves 4
Calories – 298, carbs – 9.6g, protein – 11.2g, fat – 14.3g

Ingredients

- 4 tbsp olive oil
- 1 tbsp rinsed capers
- 500g tomatoes
- A handful of fresh basil leaves
- 55g stoned and sliced olives
- Half a sliced red onion
- 1 tbsp red wine vinegar
- 300g sourdough bread, cut into small pieces
- Salt and pepper for seasoning

Method

1. Take a food processer and add the basil, oil and capers, combining well
2. Place half of the mixture into a large bowl and add the bread, coasting well
3. Take a large bowl and add most of the tomatoes, giving them a good squeeze to let out the juice
4. Add most of the olives and most of the red onion and add a little oil
5. Combine well
6. Add the bread, along with the caper mixture and vinegar, combing well until the bread is soaking up the liquid
7. Take a serving plate and add the rest of the tomatoes, olives and red onion
8. Pour the mixture over the plate and season to serve

Orange & Fennel Salad

Serves 4

Calories – 170, carbs – 10g, protein – 3g, fat – 12g

Ingredients

- 4 tbsp olive oil
- 2 fennel bulbs
- 1 large orange
- 2 tsp sherry vinegar
- 2 courgettes
- 1 small lettuce, washed
- Juice of half a lemon

Method

1. Remove the peel from the orange and cut into slices, keeping the juice that runs onto the board
2. Take the outside of the fennel away and remove the cores
3. Cut into halves and then smaller pieces
4. Use a vegetable peeler to cut the courgette into thin slices
5. Add the loose orange juice, olive oil and sherry vinegar into a small mixing bowl and combine, adding the lemon juice and combining again
6. Take a large bowl and combine the orange slices with the lettuce, fennel and courgette
7. Pour the dressing over the top and combine again

Hearty Tomato Soup

Serves 4

Calories – 212, carbs – 24g, protein – 11g, fat – 7g

Ingredients

- 1 vegetable stock cube
- 2 tbsp chopped garlic
- 50g ricotta
- 1 can of chopped tomatoes
- 400g vegetable mixture (frozen)
- A handful of fresh basil leaves
- 200ml of water

Method

1. Take a large pan and add half the vegetables and garlic, combining well and cooking over a high heat for around 5 minutes
2. Add the tomatoes, stock cube, basil and 200ml of water
3. Take a hand blender and combine until smooth
4. Add the rest of the vegetables and place a lid over the pan, cooking for another 20 minutes
5. Serve the soup with a spoonful of ricotta on top per person

Traditional Acquacotta

Serves 4
Calories – 239, carbs – 17g, protein – 14g, fat – 12g

Ingredients

- 3 tbsp olive oil
- 2 chopped carrots
- 3 chopped celery sticks
- 2 chopped garlic cloves
- 1 chopped red onion
- 2 tsp thyme (fresh or dried)
- 2 tbsp chopped fresh parsley
- 6 medium eggs
- 1 can of plum tomatoes
- 850ml chicken stock
- 50g dried mushrooms (porcini are the best)
- 3 slices of crusty-style bread, shredded

Method

1. Take a large pan and add the oil over a medium heat
2. Add the onion, carrots, celery, thyme and garlic and cook for 15 minutes
3. Add the mushrooms to a large bowl and cover with hot water for 15 minutes. Once soaked, drain the liquid and keep it to one side
4. Chop the mushrooms and add to the saucepan
5. Combine everything week and cook for 5 minutes
6. Add the tomatoes and cook for another 10 minutes
7. Add the stock and turn the heat down to a simmer
8. Meanwhile, poach the eggs in a different pan until they've set
9. Add the bread and the parsley to the saucepan and combine well
10. Serve in a bowl with a poached egg on top

Spanish Chilled Soup

Serves 4

Calories – 236, carbs – 12g, protein – 3g, fat – 20g

Ingredients

- 3 tbsp cider vinegar
- 75ml olive oil
- 8 large, chopped tomatoes
- 3 chopped garlic cloves
- 1 chopped green pepper (seeds removed)
- 2 slices of wholewheat bread
- Half a chopped red onion
- 1 egg (boiled)
- 50g chopped Serrano ham
- 100ml water

Method

1. Take a small dish and soak the bread in water for around 30 seconds
2. Turn the bread over and soak for another 30 seconds on the other side
3. Take a food processer and add the bread, green pepper, olive oil, tomatoes, and garlic, blitzing until smooth
4. Add the cider vinegar, a little salt and 100ml of water
5. Blitz once more until everything is combined and smooth
6. Place the soup in the refrigerator for around an hour
7. When you're ready to serve, drizzle with a small amount of olive oil and add the ham, onion and sliced boiled egg on top

Spicy Pesto Pasta

Serves 4
Calories – 636, carbs – 84g, protein – 22g, fat – 23g

Ingredients

- 2 tbsp olive oil
- 400g wholewheat pasta
- 6 garlic cloves, roasted and skin removed
- 4 red peppers, roasted
- 50g chopped parmesan cheese
- 1 tsp cayenne pepper
- 75g chopped blanched almonds

Method

1. Take a food processer and add the peppers, cayenne, almonds, garlic, oil and parmesan until chunky yet smooth. Season if you need to and combine
2. Cook the pasta according to instructions and drain, reserving a little of the water
3. Add the pasta back into the pan and add the pesto mixture on top, with just enough for the pasta cooking water to loosen the mixture
4. Combine everything well and serve

Dinner Recipes

Spicy Seafood Rice

Serves 4

Calories – 556, carbs – 63g, protein – 32g, fat – 14g

Ingredients

- 4 tbsp olive oil
- 1.3 litres chicken stock
- 12 prawns with the shells left on
- 4 sliced baby squid
- 300g cleaned, fresh mussels
- 1 whole garlic clove
- 3 chopped garlic cloves
- 1 chopped onion
- 1 tsp crushed fennel seeds
- 1 tsp smoked paprika
- 2 chopped celery sticks
- 300g wholewheat paella rice
- A handful of chopped parsley
- 250ml dry white wine
- 2 tbsp tomato puree

Method

1. Take a large, high-sided frying pan and 1 tbsp of the olive oil
2. Take the whole garlic clove and smash it, adding it to the pan
3. Add the prawns and cook for 2 minutes, until they're ink
4. Push the contents of the pan to one side and add the squid, cooking for another minute
5. Remove the contents of the pan to a plate and leave to one side
6. Add the rest of the oil to the same pan and cook the celery and onion for around 15 minutes, over a low to medium heat
7. Add the chopped garlic, tomato puree, paprika, and fennel seeds, combining and cooking for another 5 minutes
8. In another large saucepan, add the stock and bring it to a simmer
9. Add the rice to the frying pan containing the onion and combine
10. Add the wine to the pan and a litre of the hot stock, combing everything and simmer for 15 minutes, giving everything a stir occasionally
11. At the point when the rice is almost done but not quite, add the prawns, mussels, and the squid
12. Add the rest of the stock and the juices from the first pan
13. Cover the pan and continue to cook until the rice is cooked and the mussels have opened up
14. If any mussels don't open, discard them
15. Serve with chopped parsley

Caponata Lamb

Serves 2

Calories – 483, carbs – 40g, protein – 34g, fat – 17g

Ingredients

- 2 tsp olive oil, plus 1 extra tsp for the lamb
- 250g lamb fillet, all fat removed
- 3 cloves of garlic
- 1 sliced red onion
- 1 sliced aubergine
- 1 sliced green pepper
- 6 halved, pitted olives
- 1 carton of passata
- 2 tsp rinsed capers
- 1 tsp balsamic vinegar
- 2 tsp chopped rosemary
- 4 halved new potatoes
- 1 bag of baby spinach

Method

1. Take two of the garlic cloves and slice them finely, grating the other one and put it aside
2. Take a large frying pan and add the oil over a medium heat
3. Add the onion and cook for 5 minutes
4. Add the aubergine and cook for another 5 minutes
5. Add the passata to the pan, then the capers, half the rosemary, the olives, and the balsamic vinegar, combining well
6. Cover the pan and cook for 15 minutes, stirring every few minutes
7. Heat your oven to 170 C
8. Take a medium saucepan and boil the potatoes for 10 minutes, raining once cooked
9. Take a small bowl and add the rest of the rosemary, a little pepper and the grated garlic, combining well
10. Rub the mixture over the lamb, ensuring it is fully coated
11. Take a small roasting tin and add the lamb inside, placing it in the oven for 20 minutes
12. Meanwhile, add the spinach to a pan and all it to wilt, removing any excess water
13. Add the rest of the garlic mixture to the passata pan and combine
14. Serve the mixture alongside the lamb

Warming Fish Stew

Serves 2

Calories – 346, carbs – 20g, protein – 42g, fat – 8g

Ingredients

- 1 tbsp olive oil
- 85g shelled king prawns (raw)
- 2 fillets of pollock, skinless and cut into large chunks
- 500ml cooked fish stock (hot)
- 1 tsp fennel seeds
- 2 diced celery sticks
- 2 diced carrots
- 2 chopped garlic cloves
- 2 sliced leeks
- 1 can of chopped tomatoes

Method

1. Take a large pan and add the oil over a medium heat
2. Add the carrots, celery, garlic, and fennel seeds, cooking for 5 minutes, until softened
3. Add the leeks, the stock and the tomatoes and combine
4. Cover the pan and bring to the boil, then turn down to a simmer for around 20 minutes. The sauce should have thickened and the vegetables should be soft
5. Add the pollock and the prawns and cook for another 2 minutes, ensuring that the prawns are cooked properly before serving

Tasty Spaghetti Meatballs

Serves 4
Calories – 473, carbs – 60g, protein – 27g, fat – 11g

Ingredients

- 1 tsp olive oil, plus another 1 tbsp for the sauce
- 280g wholewheat spaghetti
- 250g minced pork, as lean as possible
- 1 can of green lentils
- 1 crushed garlic clove
- Half a tsp chopped rosemary
- Half a tsp Dijon mustard
- 2 chopped shallots
- 2 chopped garlic cloves
- 2 tsp tomato puree
- 500g halved cherry tomatoes
- 1 tsp chilli flakes
- 125ml water

Method

1. Preheat your oven to 200 C
2. Take a baking sheet and line it with foil and then brush over with 1 tsp of olive oil
3. Take the lentils and empty them into a bowl, using a fork to crush them down a little
4. Take a large bowl and add the lentils, the pork, crushed garlic clove, rosemary, garlic and a little seasoning, combining well
5. Separate the mixture into four even sections, and from those sections create 5 meatballs – you should have a total of 20 meatballs
6. Place the meatballs on the baking sheet and give them a roll around in the oil to coat
7. Cook for 15 minutes, until brown and soft, setting aside
8. Take a large frying pan and add 2 tsp of the oil over a medium heat
9. Add the garlic and shallots and cook for 4 minutes
10. Add the rest of the oil and the tomatoes, ensuring that they're laid with the cut side on the pan
11. Add the water and the tomato puree, combining lightly so as not to squash the tomatoes
12. Turn the heat down to a simmer for 2 minutes
13. Add the oregano, chilli flakes and a little seasoning and combine
14. Take a regular casserole dish and pour the sauce inside
15. Add the cooked meatballs and ladle the sauce over the meatballs
16. Cover the dish with foil and place in the oven for 10 minutes
17. Meanwhile, cook the spaghetti according to instructions and drain
18. Place the spaghetti on the plate with the meatballs and sauce on top

Fishy Vegetable Traybake

Serves 2
Calories – 387, carbs – 28g, protein – 28g, fat – 17g

Ingredients

- 2 tbsp olive oil
- Cooking spray
- 2 fillets of seabass
- 300g sliced potatoes
- 1 sliced red pepper
- Half a sliced lemon
- 25g halved, pitted olives
- 1 chopped spring of rosemary
- A few basil leaves

Method

1. Preheat your oven to 180 C
2. Take a baking tray and spray with a little cooking spray
3. Arrange the peppers and potatoes on the tray
4. Add 1 tbsp of the oil over the top and the rosemary, season and give everything a shake and a toss
5. Place in the oven for 25 minutes, stopping halfway to turn over
6. Place the fish on top of the baked vegetables and the olives
7. On top of each fish fillet, add a lemon slice
8. Cook for another 8 minutes, ensuring the fish is cooked all the way through
9. Add a few shredded basil leaves on top before serving

Herby Chicken Paella

Serves 4
Calories – 660, carbs – 79g, protein – 41g, fat – 20g

Ingredients

- 3 tbsp olive oil
- 6 chicken thighs
- 1.5 litres of chicken stock
- 2 chopped onions
- 3 sliced garlic cloves
- 2 tbsp plain flour
- 400g wholewheat paella rice
- 0.5 tsp saffron
- 1 tsp sweet paprika
- The juice and zest from 2 lemons
- 200g frozen peas
- A handful of chopped mint leaves
- A handful of chopped dill leaves
- A handful of chopped parsley leaves

Method

1. Preheat your oven to 180 C
2. Arrange the chicken thighs on your countertop and season them with salt and pepper
3. Dust over the chicken thighs with flour and ensure that both sides are covered
4. Take a large, deep frying pan and add 1 tbsp of the oil
5. Cook the chicken thighs until browned and then place in a roasting tin
6. Place in the oven to finish cooking for up to 40 minutes
7. Add the rest of the oil to the same frying pan and cook the garlic and onions for around 15 minutes
8. Add the paprika, zest, saffron and the rice and combine
9. Add the stock and turn down to a simmer, stirring every soft often for about 20 minutes
10. When the rice is almost cooked, add the peas and beans and the lemon juice, stirring well
11. Remove from the heat and add the chicken thighs to the pan
12. Cover for 5 minutes before serving

Fennel Stuffed Fish

Serves 4
Calories – 489, carbs – 45g, protein – 36g, fat – 18g

Ingredients

- 2 whole seabass
- 3 tbsp olive oil
- 1 sliced onion
- 2 sliced fennel bulbs
- 200g couscous
- The zest of one lemon
- 1 lemon cut into wedges
- 250g halved tomatoes
- 1 tbsp currants
- 250ml chicken stock (you can also use vegetable stock)
- 2 tbsp toasted pine nuts
- A handful of chopped dill

Method

1. Preheat your oven to 200 C
2. Take a large roasting tin and add the onion and fennel with 2 tbsp of the oil, tossing well and seasoning
3. Place in the oven for 20 minutes
4. Take a medium mixing bowl and add the couscous
5. Pour the stock over the bowl and cover over with some cling film for 10 minutes
6. Cut two deep slits into the sides of the fish and season with pepper, salt and a little lemon zest
7. Take the couscous and use a fork to fluff it up
8. Add 2 tbsp of the lemon juice, the rest of the zest, 1 tbsp of the pine nuts, seasoning and the dill, combining well
9. Take the mixture and place it inside the fish, via the deep slits you cut into the sides
10. Take the roasting tin you used earlier and add the currants and tomatoes, stirring into the juices
11. Place the fish on top and cook for 30 minutes, ensuring the fish is fully cooked
12. Cover with the pine nuts and use the tin for serving, alongside the lemon wedges
13. Use any leftover couscous as a side dish

Cheesy Spinach Chicken

Serves 4
Calories – 352, carbs – 32g, protein – 39g, fat – 8g

Ingredients

- ⏣ 1 tbsp olive oil
- ⏣ 85g cream cheese
- ⏣ 4 chicken breasts
- ⏣ 1 sliced onion
- ⏣ 20 cherry tomatoes
- ⏣ 200g pre-thawed frozen chicken, chopped
- ⏣ 500g sliced potato
- ⏣ 4 sliced garlic cloves
- ⏣ 8 chopped black olives
- ⏣ A pinch of grated nutmeg

Method

1. Preheat the oven to 220 C
2. Take a large baking sheet and line with baking parchment
3. Take a mixing bowl and add the onion, covering over with boiling water
4. Leave the bowl to soak for 15 minutes
5. Take another bowl and add the spinach, cheese and nutmeg and combine well
6. Spread the mixture over the chicken breasts
7. Place the tomatoes over the top
8. Take the onion and drain the water
9. Place the potatoes, onion, garlic, oil, and olives into another mixing bowl and season well, tossing to coat
10. Place the potatoes onto the parchment and flatten out
11. Place in the oven for 25 minutes
12. Once cooked, arrange the potatoes into four piles and place a chicken breast on top of each one
13. Place back into the oven for another 20 minutes, making sure that the chicken is fully cooked

Lentil & Aubergine "Lasagne"

Serves 4
Calories – 359, carbs – 34g, protein – 19g, fat – 16g

Ingredients

- 3 tbsp olive oil
- 140g lentils
- 2 aubergines, cut lengthways
- 3 chopped garlic cloves
- 2 chopped onions
- 125g torn mozzarella
- 1 can of tomatoes
- 300g butternut squash, cooked
- Half a pack of basil leaves

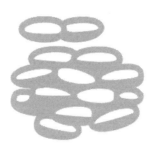

Method

1. Preheat the oven to 220 C
2. Take the aubergine and brush each side with 2 tbsp of olive oil
3. Take a large baking sheet and arrange the aubergines on top, seasoning to your liking
4. Cook in the oven for 20 minutes, turning at the halfway point
5. Cook the lentils according to instructions
6. Take a large frying pan and add the rest of the oil
7. Add the onions and garlic and cook for a few minutes, until softened
8. Add the butternut squash and the tomatoes, along with a little water to loosen
9. Cook for 15 minutes until a thickened sauce appears
10. Add the basil and lentils and combine
11. Season to your liking
12. Take a small baking dish and add a layer of the lentil mixture
13. Add the aubergine slices on top and add another layer of lentils, then aubergines, repeating until you've run out of ingredients
14. Add the mozzarella on top and cook for 15 minutes

Peppery Steak Salad

Serves 2

Calories – 498, carbs – 48g, protein – 38g, fat – 17g

Ingredients

- 1 tbsp olive oil
- 300g lean steak
- 85g rinsed pearl barley
- 1 chopped red pepper
- 1 chopped yellow pepper
- 1 red onion cut into wedges
- The juice of half a lemon
- Half a bag of watercress

Method

1. Cook the pearl barley according to instructions
2. Drain and place the barley into a bowl
3. Preheat your oven to 200 C
4. Take a baking tray and add the wedges of onion
5. Add 1 tbsp of olive oil and toss to coat the onion
6. Cook in the oven for 20 minutes
7. Take the steak and season, rubbing a little oil over both sides
8. Take a large frying pan and cook on both sides for around 4 minutes each
9. Remove the steak from the pan and allow to rest
10. Add the onions and peppers to the pearl barley and combine
11. Add the lemon juice, seasoning and the watercress and combine once more
12. Take the steak and cut into thin slices
13. Arrange the steak on top of the salad

Dessert Recipes

Mediterranean Apple Cake

Serves 12
Calories – 450, carbs – 34g, protein – 13g, fat – 24g

Ingredients

- 380g wholewheat flour
- 2 large apples, peeled and chopped into small pieces
- 128g sugar
- 2 large eggs
- 95g raisins
- Juice from two large oranges
- 0.5 tsp cinnamon
- 0.5 tsp nutmeg
- 1 tsp baking powder
- 1 tsp baking soda
- 230ml olive oil

Method

1. Preheat your oven to 220 C
2. Take a large bowl and add the apples, pouring the orange juice over the top, just enough to cover
3. Take another mixing bowl and sift the cinnamon, nutmeg, flour, baking soda and baking powder. Place the bowl to one side
4. Mix together the olive oil and sugar using a stand mixer
5. Whilst mixing, slowly add the eggs and mix for another 2 minutes
6. Take the bowl containing the dry ingredients and create a hole in the middle
7. Add the egg mixture into that hole and use a wooden spoon to stir carefully
8. Drain the apples and add the apples and the raisins to the mixture
9. Combine with a wooden spoon
10. Take a 9" cake tin and line with parchment paper
11. Add the batter into the tin and level off the top
12. Place in the oven for 45 minutes, until the centre is cooked

Healthier Brownies

Serves 8
Calories – 480, carbs – 46g, protein – 34g, fat – 28g

Ingredients

- 59ml olive oil
- 32g Greek yogurt
- 2 eggs
- 1 tsp vanilla extract
- 64g flour
- 96g sugar
- 0.5 tsp baking powder
- Pinch of salt
- 50g cocoa powder
- 20g chopped walnuts

Method

1. Preheat your oven to 220 C
2. Take a mixing bowl and add the sugar and olive oil, mixing everything together well
3. Add the vanilla and mix again
4. Take a small mixing bowl and add the eggs, beating until smooth
5. Add the other mixture and combine
6. Pour the yogurt into the mixture and combine again
7. Take another bowl and add the cocoa powder, flour, baking powder, and the salt, combining
8. Add to the other mixture and combine again
9. Add the nuts and combine once more
10. Take a square 9" baking tin and line with parchment paper
11. Pour the mixture into the pan and smooth the top
12. Place in the oven and cook for 25 minutes
13. Once cooled, cut into squares

Smooth Chocolate Mousse

Serves 4
Calories – 328, carbs – 25g, protein – 15.8g, fat – 9.8g

Ingredients

- 100g dark chocolate
- 180ml milk
- 500ml Greek yogurt
- 1tbsp honey
- 0.5 tsp vanilla extract

Method

1. Take a large saucepan and add the milk and chocolate
2. Heat very lightly, until the chocolate melts and don't allow it to boil
3. Add the honey and vanilla and combine well
4. Take a large mixing bowl and add the chocolate mixture
5. Combine well and share between serving bowls
6. Place the bowls in the refrigerator for at least 2 hours

Banana & Peanut Butter Bowls

Serves 4
Calories – 370, carbs – 47g, protein – 22g, fat – 10g

Ingredients

- 2 sliced bananas
- 900ml Greek yogurt
- 1 tsp nutmeg
- 32g peanut butter
- 32g flax seed meal

Method

1. Take four bowls and divide the yogurt between them
2. Add sliced banana on top
3. Take the peanut butter and melt in the microwave or over a low heat on the hob
4. Place one tablespoon of the peanut butter over the top of each bowl
5. Add a little flax seed meal and nutmeg on top of each bowl

Honey Yogurt With Balsamic Berries

Serves 4
Calories – 230, carbs – 15g, protein – 11g, fat – 14g

Ingredients

- 8 quartered strawberries
- 1 tbsp balsamic vinegar
- 128g raspberries
- 128g blueberries
- 2 tsp honey
- 157ml Greek yogurt

Method

1. Take a large bowl and add the berries and balsamic vinegar
2. Combine and allow to rest for 10 minutes
3. Take a small bowl and add the honey and yogurt, combining well
4. Take four serving bowls and divide the berries equally between them
5. Place a large serving of the yogurt on top of each one

Creamy Ricotta Brule

Serves 4
Calories – 330, carbs – 35g, protein – 35g, fat – 23g

Ingredients

- 260g ricotta cheese
- 1 tbsp lemon zest
- 2 tbsp sugar
- 2 tbsp honey

Method

1. Take a large bowl and add the lemon zest, honey and ricotta, combining well
2. Take four ramekin dishes and divide the mixture equally between them
3. Place the dishes on a baking sheet and sprinkle over the top with a little sugar
4. Place in the oven or under the grill for between 5-10 minutes
5. The tops should be extremely hot and brown
6. Allow to cool for 10 minutes before serving

Nutty Shortbread

Serves 8
Calories – 400, carbs – 15g, protein – 11g, fat – 32g

Ingredients

- 118ml olive oil
- 150g hazelnut meal
- 125g flour
- 1 tsp salt
- Zest and juice of 1 lemon
- 1 tsp vanilla
- 40g brown sugar
- 40g powdered sugar
- Pinch of salt

Method

1. Preheat your oven to 230 C
2. Take a large bowl and combine the flour, hazelnut meal, sugar, a quarter of the powdered sugar, lemon zest and a little salt
3. Whisk the olive oil and vanilla into the mixture
4. Take an 8x8" baking dish and press the dough inside
5. Place in the oven for 20 minutes
6. Cut the shortbread into squares once out of the oven
7. Allow to cool before removing from the baking dish
8. Take a small bowl and combine the lemon juice with the powdered sugar and pour over the cookies whilst still warm

Vanilla Pears

Serves 4
Calories – 250, carbs – 12g, protein – 7g, fat – 22g

Ingredients

- 4 large pears
- 120ml maple syrup (pure is best)
- 0.25 tsp cinnamon
- 1 tsp vanilla extract

Method

1. Preheat your oven to 190 C
2. Take a baking sheet and line with baking parchment
3. Take the pears and cut them into halves. Cut a small amount of the underside away, so they stand up on the baking tray
4. Use a teaspoon to scoop out the middle of the pears and remove the seeds
5. Arrange the pears on the baking sheet, with the middles facing upwards
6. Sprinkle the cinnamon over the top of each pear
7. Take a small bowl and combine the vanilla and maple syrup
8. Drizzle the mixture over the pears, keeping a small amount to one side for after the pears have cooked
9. Place the pears in the oven for 25 minutes. The pears should be browned and soft
10. Whilst they're still hot, drizzle the rest of the syrup over the top and serve whilst still warm

Strawberry Ice Lollies

Serves 8
Calories – 124, carbs – 8g, protein – 3g, fat – 15g

Ingredients

- 150ml almond milk
- 300g strawberries

Method

1. Take the strawberries and wash them well, patting dry
2. Remove the hull of the strawberries and cut into quarters
3. Place the strawberries into the blender, followed by the almond milk
4. Blend until smooth
5. Take small popsicle moulds and pour the mixture inside
6. Place in the freezer for at least four hours

Mediterranean Chocolate Chip Cookies

Serves 12

Calories – 280, carbs – 13g, protein – 12g, fat – 22g

Ingredients

- 100g olive oil
- 80g tahini
- 100g brown sugar
- The juice of one orange
- 1 tbsp flax seeds
- 2 tsp vanilla extract
- 200g wholewheat flour
- 0.5 tsp cinnamon
- 0.5 tsp baking soda
- 0.5 tsp espresso coffee powder
- 150g chocolate, chopped into small pieces
- Pinch of salt

Method

1. Place the flax seeds in a bowl with the orange juice and place to one side

2. Take a large mixing bowl and add the oil, tahini, orange juice mixture, brown sugar, cinnamon, espresso powder, and vanilla, combining well. Add the salt and combine again Make sure that the sugar has mostly dissolved

3. Take another bowl and mix the baking soda with the flour

4. Add the flour to the mixture and use a spatula to fold in carefully

5. Add the chocolate and combine everything well

6. Place the bowl in the refrigerator for around 4 hours

7. Preheat your oven to 185 C

8. Take a baking sheet and line it with parchment paper

9. Take your dough out of the refrigerator and divide into 12 pieces

10. Use your hands to roll the pieces into balls and place onto the baking tray. Make sure you leave some space between for spreading

11. Place in the oven for 11 minutes and allow the cookies to cool and set a little

14 Days Meal Plan

Now you've seen how delicious the Mediterranean Diet can be, it's time to look towards the practical side of things.

The recipes we've given you so far are easy to make, full of ingredients which you'll have no problems finding in the supermarket, and they won't break the bank either. Not only that, but these recipes are packed with vitamins and minerals, including all the nutrition you need for a healthy mind, body, and soul.

However, whenever you start a new eating regime, it's a good idea to have a plan to get you started. It's easy to become confused or accidentally start eating too much of the wrong thing from the start. That's why we've put together a handy 14 days plan to get you off to the best possible start in your Mediterranean Diet journey.

Below you'll find 14 days' worth of meals, including a breakfast, lunch, and dinner. You'll notice that we included a dessert section in the book, and if you feel like enjoying a dessert on any given day, you can incorporate that too, provided you stick to either the recipes we've given you, or you make sure that whatever you have is made of fresh, Mediterranean Diet-approved ingredients and that it's not packed with a huge amount of fat or sugar.

Remember to drink plenty of water every single day and if you want to, you can have one small glass of wine. If you don't like one particular meal, we've shown you for a particular day, that's fine. You can mix and match however you like, but make sure that you stay within the guidelines we talked about in our introductory section, to avoid accidentally moving into the 'unhealthy 'realm'.

The great thing about the Mediterranean diet is that it's not only packed with delicious meals, but that it's also very flexible. Once you've got the basics down-pat, you'll find it easy to mix and match and find meals which fit the guidelines and offer you delicious alternatives to the types of foods that perhaps you don't like so much.

So, if you're ready, let's get started with day 1 of your Mediterranean journey!

Day 1

Breakfast – Artichoke & spinach breakfast frittata (See page 14)
Lunch – Baked Flatbread With Falafel
Serves 9
Calories – 130, carbs – 19g, protein – 6g, fat – 1g

Ingredients

- 1 tbsp olive oil
- 128g soaked chickpeas
- 70g chopped onion
- 70g chickpea flour
- 3 tbsp water
- 70g chopped cilantro
- 128g chopped parsley
- 3 cloves of garlic
- 1 chopped green pepper
- 1 tsp salt
- 1 tsp cumin
- 0.25 tsp pepper
- 0.5 tsp cardamom
- 0.5 tsp baking soda

Method

1. Preheat your oven to 220 C
2. Take the chickpeas and drain away the liquid
3. Place the chickpeas into a food processor

4. Add the pepper, salt, green pepper cumin, garlic, cardamom, onion, cilantro, parsley, and baking soda to the food processor and combine well until you get a grainy mixture

5. Pour the mixture into a large mixing bowl and place in the refrigerator for an hour

6. Once chilled, add the water, flour, oil and chickpea flour to the mixture and combine everything using your hands

7. Take a baking sheet and line with parchment paper

8. Pour the mixture onto the sheet and press it down with your hands to create a completely flat surface

9. Place in the oven for 25 minutes

10. Once cooked, allow the bread to cool for around 10 minutes before slicing up

Dinner – Spicy seafood rice (See page 50)

Day 2

Breakfast – Toast, sweet potato style
Serves 2
Calories – 22, carbs – 5g, protein – 1g, fat – 1g

Ingredients

- A dash of olive oil
- 1 large sweet potato

Method

1. Preheat your oven to 220 C
2. Take the sweet potato and cut into slices, around half an inch thick
3. Take a baking sheet and line with baking parchment
4. Place the potato slices onto the baking sheet, leaving a small amount of space between
5. Drizzle the potato slices with a small amount of oil
6. Place in the oven for half an hour, making sure that they're cooked through
7. Serve whilst still warm

Lunch – Simple pasta salad (See page 32)
Dinner – Caponata lamb (See page 52)

Day 3

Breakfast – Breakfast shakshuka (See page 16)
Lunch – Healthy tuna wraps (See page 35)
Dinner – Balsamic & vegetable chicken

Serves 4
Calories – 441, carbs – 15g, protein – 20g, fat – 32g

Ingredients

- 4 tbsp olive oil
- 4 chicken thighs
- 1 tbsp maple syrup
- 2 minced garlic cloves
- 1 red onion
- 100ml balsamic vinegar
- 12 brussels sprouts
- Salt and pepper for seasoning

Method

1. Take a small mixing bowl and use a whisk to combine the balsamic vinegar, maple syrup, garlic, seasoning and 2 tbsp olive oil
2. Add the chicken thighs to a large bowl and pour the mixture on top, making sure they're well coated
3. Cover the chicken with plastic wrap and place in the refrigerator for 2 hours
4. Preheat your oven to 220 C
5. Cut the brussels sprouts into halves and the red onion into chunks
6. Take a large baking sheet and arrange the brussels sprouts and the onions on top
7. Drizzle with the rest of the olive oil and season, making sure everything is tossed to coat

8. Take the chicken out of the bowl and place on the baking sheet, arranging the vegetables around it

9. Place in the oven for half an hour, making sure that the chicken is fully cooked

10. Meanwhile, add the mixture from the chicken bowl into a small saucepan, over a medium heat

11. Allow the mixture to simmer for around 10 minutes, creating a thickened and reduced sauce

12. Brush the mixture over the chicken as it's cooking and return to the oven

13. Serve once the chicken is cooked

Day 4

Breakfast – Sprout & sweet potato hash (See page 18)
Lunch – Delicious butternut squash soup

Serves 4
Calories – 292, carbs – 54g, protein – 4g, fat – 4g

Ingredients

- 🍽 1 tbsp avocado oil
- 🍽 1 large butternut squash
- 🍽 1 peeled clove of garlic
- 🍽 1 halved onion
- 🍽 0.5 tbsp maple syrup
- 🍽 0.25 tsp nutmeg
- 🍽 0.25 tsp ginger
- 🍽 900ml vegetable broth
- 🍽 Salt and pepper for seasoning

Method

1. Preheat your oven to 250 C
2. Take the butternut squash and slice off the ends and then turn to slice lengthways, into halves
3. Take a large spoon and scoop out the membrane and the seeds
4. Take a baking tray and add the butternut squash with the inside facing upwards
5. Season with salt and pepper and then turn the butternut squash over and place in the oven for 1 hour

6. Halfway through cooking, place the onion halves onto the tray, coat in a little toil and cook for the remaining half an hour

7. Allow the butternut squash to cool a little and once you can handle it, scoop out the flesh with a spoon. This needs to be placed into a blender

8. Take the middle of the onion out and also add that to the blender

9. Add the maple syrup, nutmeg, ginger, garlic and broth to the blender and pulse to achieve a creamy mixture

10. Check the taste and season if required

11. Serve with a little black pepper on top

Dinner – Peppery steak salad (See page 66)

Day 5

Breakfast – Super-versatile oatmeal
Serves 1
Calories – 260, carbs – 36g, protein – 12g, fat – 1g

Ingredients

- 230ml water (you can use milk if you want a creamier consistency)
- 70g rolled oats
- A pinch of salt

Method

1. Take a saucepan and add the water (or milk), bringing it to a boil
2. Once the water (or milk) starts to boil, add the oats and combine well
3. Turn the heat down to allow the mixture to simmer for around 5 minutes, or a little longer if you like the oatmeal thicker, stirring as it cooks
4. Once cooked, add any filling you like. You can add berries, seeds, or even eggs on top!

Lunch – Fully stuffed peppers (See page 33)
Dinner – Warming fish stew (See page 54)

Day 6

Breakfast – Scrambled eggs, Med style (See page 20)
Lunch – Vegetable couscous with halloumi cheese (See page 37)
Dinner – Ginger scallops with a hint of citrus

Serves 4

Calories – 254, carbs – 12g, protein – 21g, fat – 13g

Ingredients

- 2 tbsp avocado oil
- The zest and juice of 1 orange
- The juice of 1 lemon
- 700g scallops
- 2 tbsp butter (you can also use ghee)
- 1 tbsp grated ginger
- Salt and pepper for seasoning

Method

1. Take the scallops and season with a little salt
2. Take a large pan and add the oil, over a medium heat
3. Once the oil is hot, add the scallops and sear for 2 minutes on each side
4. Take the scallops out of the pan and place on a plate

5. Turn the heat down a little and add the lemon juice, orange zest, butter, and ginger, combining well and allowing the mixture to simmer

6. Once it is simmering, add the scallops and use a spoon to cover them with the sauce

7. Serve the scallops on a plate with the sauce poured over the top

Day 7

Breakfast – Mediterranean morning casserole (See page 21)
Lunch – Salmon burgers
Serves 2 (2 burgers each)
Calories – 420, carbs – 6.3g, protein – 25g, fat – 33g

Ingredients

- 450g salmon (fresh is always best)
- 4 tbsp olive oil
- 1 diced red pepper
- 1 diced onion
- 2 beaten eggs
- 2 minced garlic cloves
- 70g almond flour
- 1 tbsp Dijon mustard
- 2 tbsp mayonnaise
- 2 tbsp chopped dill
- 25g chopped parsley
- Salt and pepper for seasoning

Method

1. Preheat your oven to 240 C
2. Place the salmon on a baking tray and drizzle a little olive oil over the top, seasoning generously
3. Cook for 13 minutes, until cooked through
4. Once cooked, cool in the refrigerator, for around 10 minutes

5. Meanwhile take a large frying pan and add 1 tbsp of the olive oil over a medium heat

6. Add the pepper and onion and cook for 8 minutes

7. Remove the vegetables from the heat and place to one side

8. Take a mixing bowl and use your hands to remove the salmon from the skin, placing the flakes of fish into the bowl

9. Add the onion, pepper, dill, mayonnaise, garlic, eggs, almond flour, mustard, and parsley and use your hands to combine everything well

10. Use your hands to form burgers, you should have four in total

11. Take a large frying pan and add the rest of the olive oil over a medium heat

12. Cook the burgers for around 4 minutes on each side

13. Blot dry with paper towels and serve whilst hot

Dinner – Tasty spaghetti meatballs (See page 55)

Day 8

Breakfast – Avocado, cucumber & salmon parcels
Serves 4 (3 parcels each)
Calories – 46, carbs – 2g, protein – 3g, fat – 3g

Ingredients

- 170g smoked salmon
- 1 cucumber
- 1 peeled avocado with pit removed
- 0.5 tbsp fresh lime juice
- Black pepper for seasoning

Method

1. Prepare a serving plate
2. Take the cucumber and slice into quarter inch thick slices
3. Place the cucumber on the plate
4. Take a mixing bowl and add the lime juice and avocado, using a fork to mash everything and form a creamy consistency
5. Add a small amount of avocado mash onto the top of each cucumber slice
6. Add a piece of smoked salmon top
7. Garnish with black pepper
8. Repeat for the rest of the cucumber slices as a base

Lunch – Fresh Panzanella (See page 39)
Dinner – Fishy vegetable traybake (See page 57)

Day 9

Breakfast – Breakfast pizza (See page 23)
Lunch – Orange & fennel salad (See page 41)
Dinner – Chicken kabobs
Serves 6
Calories – 135, carbs – 11g, protein – 10g, fat – 1g

Ingredients

- 4 tbsp olive oil
- 680g chicken breasts (boneless and skinless)
- 3 tbsp fresh lemon juice
- 1 tsp Dijon mustard
- 2 tbsp red wine vinegar
- 1 tsp oregano (dried)
- 3 minced garlic cloves
- 1 sliced red bell pepper
- 1 sliced yellow bell pepper
- 1 sliced zucchini
- 1 sliced red onion
- Salt and pepper for seasoning

Method

1. Take a small mixing bowl and combine the red wine vinegar, olive oil, Dijon mustard, lemon juice, garlic, oregano and seasoning
2. Cut your chicken breasts into chunks and place in a glass bowl
3. Cover the chicken with the marinade and make sure everything is covered
4. Cover over with plastic wrap and place in the refrigerator for one hour
5. Heat your grill to a medium heat
6. Take metal skewers and alternate between chicken, onion, pepper, and zucchini
7. Place your skewers onto the grill and cook for 7 minutes on each side, making sure that the chicken is fully cooked

Day 10

Breakfast – Hummus with cauliflower fritters (See page 25)

Lunch – Vibrant beetroot soup

Serves 4

Calories – 145, carbs – 19g, protein – 2g, fat – 1g

Ingredients

- 2 tbsp olive oil
- 940g vegetable broth
- 1 tbsp chopped ginger (fresh)
- 1 onion
- 3 minced garlic clovers
- 3 peeled and diced beetroots
- 1 peeled and diced parsnip
- Salt and pepper for seasoning

Method

1. Take a large soup pot and add the olive oil over a medium heat
2. Cook the onion until soft, for around 5 minutes
3. Add the ginger, garlic, and seasoning and cook for another 2 minutes
4. Add the parsnips, beetroot and broth, combining well
5. Bring the mixture to a boil and then turn down to a simmer for half an hour, covering the pot
6. Once cooked and the beetroot is soft, place the soup into a blender and blend until you reach the consistency you like
7. Serve with salt and pepper as a seasoning

Dinner – Herby chicken paella (See page 58)

Day 11

Breakfast – Delicious morning yogurt
Serves 7
Calories – 103, carbs – 8g, protein – 5g, fat – 3g

Ingredients

- 1 packet of regular yogurt starter (available in health stores)
- 1200g organic milk

Method

1. Take a large microwave-safe bowl and add the milk inside
2. Place the bowl into the microwave and use a high setting. Use a thermometer and cook until the milk reaches 82 C
3. Remove from the microwave and allow until it reaches 46 C
4. Take a small glass and pour 230ml of the milk inside
5. Add the yogurt starter and combine well
6. Pour the contents of the glass back into the main milk bowl and combine well
7. Take your yogurt maker and fill up the glasses, setting your timer for 9 hours
8. Once the 9 hours have passed, take the glasses out of the machine and place into the refrigerator
9. You can serve your homemade, healthy yogurt with berries, granola, or simply eat on its own

Lunch – Hearty tomato soup (See page 42)
Lunch – Hearty tomato soup (See page 42)
Dinner – Fennel stuffed fish (See page 60)
Dinner – Fennel stuffed fish (See page 60)

Day 12

Breakfast – Delicious breakfast quinoa (See page 27)
Lunch – Traditional acquacotta (See page 43)
Dinner – Fennel & pork balls

Serves 8

Calories – 95, carbs – 9g, protein – 4g, fat – 2g

Ingredients

- 900g ground pork
- 5.5 tbsp olive oil
- Half a chopped onion
- 1 chopped fennel bulb (split into two halves)
- 15g chopped parsley
- 2 beaten eggs
- 1 tsp fennel seeds
- 120g baby spinach
- 4 chopped garlic cloves
- Salt and pepper for seasoning

Method

1. Take a large frying pan and add 1 tbsp of the olive oil over a medium heat
2. Add half the fennel and the onion and cook for 3 minutes
3. Remove from the pan and place to one side to cool
4. Take a large bowl and add the meat, parsley, fennel seeds, eggs, and seasoning, along with the cooled fennel and onion

5. Use your hands to combine all the ingredients well
6. Create balls out of the mixture, giving you around 35 balls in total
7. Take a baking tray and line with baking paper
8. Place the meatballs onto a sheet of parchment paper whilst they're waiting
9. Take a large frying pan and add 4 tbsp of olive oil, over a medium heat
10. Place the meatballs into the pan, leaving a little space in-between. You will probably have to do this in batches, depending upon the size of your pan
11. Cook for 3 minutes on each side and blot on a paper towel
12. Meanwhile, take a medium frying pan and add the rest of the olive oil over a medium heat
13. Add the rest of the fennel and cook for 5 minutes
14. Add the garlic and cook for 2 more minutes, and then add the spinach, combining well
15. Serve the spinach and fennel mixture alongside the meatballs

Day 13

Breakfast – Caprese breakfast muffin (See page 28)
Lunch – Sauté-style cabbage

Serves 6
Calories – 80, carbs – 9g, protein – 2g, fat – 5g

Ingredients

- 2 tbsp ghee
- 1 thinly sliced cabbage head
- 2 minced garlic cloves
- 1 sliced onion
- Salt and pepper for seasoning

Method

1. Take the cabbage and cut into half, removing the middle and cutting into slices
2. Take a large skillet and add the ghee, over a medium heat
3. Add the onion and cook for 1 minute
4. Add the garlic and cook for a further minute, combining well
5. Add the cabbage and cook for 15 minutes, siring every so often
6. The cabbage will soften and eventually will caramelise
7. Serve with salt and pepper

Dinner – Cheesy spinach chicken (See page 62)

Day 14

Breakfast – Frittata with smoked salmon
Serves 6
Calories – 326, carbs – 7.8g, protein – 23g, fat – 22g

Ingredients

- 3 tbsp olive oil
- 226g smoked salmon, cut into small pieces
- 3 sliced scallions
- 1 diced shallot
- 1 diced leek
- 246g yogurt
- 10 eggs
- 1 bunch of chopped parsley
- 1 bunch of chopped dill
- 113g goat's cheese
- Salt and pepper for seasoning

Method

1. Take a large skillet and add 1 tbsp of the olive oil over a medium heat
2. Add the shallot, scallions and leek and cook for 2 minutes
3. Remove the contents of the pan and place to one side
4. Take a large mixing bowl and add the yogurt and eggs, combining well with a whisk
5. Add the herbs, goat's cheese, leek, shallot, and scallions, along with the salmon and combine well, seasoning to your taste

6. Add 2 tbsp of olive oil to the same skillet and pour the mixture inside
7. Cook for 10 minutes, until the edges are setting
8. Remove the skillet from the hob and place under the grill, cooking for another 10 minutes
9. Cut into slices and serve

Lunch – Spicy pesto pasta (See page 47)
Dinner – Lentil & aubergine "lasagne" (See page 64)

Conclusion

And there we have it, your introduction to the wonders of the Mediterranean Diet. Everything you've learned in this book will set you up for your new journey into a healthier lifestyle and the benefits are far-reaching.

Those who live in the Mediterranean region may find it easier to get hold of fresh, organic ingredients, grown in the delicious sunlight of the fertile Mediterranean lands, but that doesn't mean that you can't have the same delicious tastes and health benefits here in the UK!

Remember to mix up your daily meals to avoid boredom and do your best to meal plan, to make your life easier and to avoid falling back into unhealthy eating patterns.

All that's left to say is good luck and enjoy your new healthy, delicious journey!

Disclaimer

This book contains opinions and ideas of the author and is meant to teach the reader informative and helpful knowledge while due care should be taken by the user in the application of the information provided. The instructions and strategies are possibly not right for every reader and there is no guarantee that they work for everyone. Using this book and implementing the information/recipes therein contained is explicitly your own responsibility and risk. This work with all its contents, does not guarantee correctness, completion, quality or correctness of the provided information. Misinformation or misprints cannot be completely eliminated.

Printed in Great Britain
by Amazon